T0067329

THE LITTLE BOOK OF BIG ENERGIZERS

Make Your Meetings More Fun, More Focused, and Simply More Fabulous!

JEANNINE MCGLADE AND **ANDREW PEK**

Order this book online at www.trafford.com
or email orders@trafford.com

Most Trafford titles are also available at major online book retailers.

Print information available on the last page.

ISBN: 978-1-4907-8717-6 (sc)
ISBN: 978-1-4907-8725-1 (e)

Library of Congress Control Number: 2018932957

Trafford rev. 01/31/2018

Trafford
PUBLISHING®   www.trafford.com
North America & international
toll-free: 1 888 232 4444 (USA & Canada)
fax: 812 355 4082

Contents

Contributions and Dedication

The authors would like to thank Ian Limbaga for his creative and stimulating illustrations and Patricia Hall for her thorough editing of the content in this (and so many other) book projects!

This book is dedicated to all of our clients past and present. Because you trusted us, we grew together, had fun, and did great work together. Thank you!

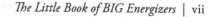

Introduction

This little book of BIG energizers is for anyone who has to facilitate or conduct any meeting, of any kind, for any length of time, for any purpose. Whether you are facilitating weekly or monthly team meetings, ideation sessions, training workshops, strategy meetings, OD interventions, any type of meeting whatsoever, this little book is for you!

Our guess is that you picked up this book to add a little fun to your meetings or kick up the energy in your meetings. Or maybe you're tired of conducting or attending so many meetings that are just either flat out boring or where you find yourself (or others!) daydreaming or doing other things! Research suggests that some of us spend up to 50% of our time each day in meetings – and hours preparing for those meetings – that's a lot of time! There are millions of meetings happening all over the world – right now, this very instant! And at most of those meetings, participants are unengaged, bored, checking their social media accounts or thinking about dinner. Not present, not happy, not focused and certainly not having any fun. So, we're spending a ton of time in meetings but are we getting the most out of the time we are spending?

We'd venture to guess the answer is a BIG "no." We aren't getting the most out of the time we are spending in meetings. Now, you know, there are many books that give strategies around how to get the most out of your meetings – important topics like meeting management, facilitation, setting expectations, writing agendas, inviting the right people, etc. But, this is NOT that book. This book has really one specific purpose. And it's simple, really – not complicated, not complex, doesn't require a meeting to implement and won't take you much time at all. The purpose is to bring more energy into your meetings. We can use many words to describe what energy is – life force, vitality, power, action, vigor, etc. And no matter what words we may use to describe what energy is, we certainly all know and have experienced the effect of energy. We've all experienced the difference between a meeting that has energy and a meeting that has no energy. We've met people with such "great energy" and those who had "no energy." We just know it when we feel it. And we know when it's missing.

Think about that for a moment. Can you remember a time when you've been to a meeting where there was just no energy? What did that feel like? What did people look like? What were people saying and doing? Chances are people were disengaged, thinking about or doing other things (not related to the meeting) and people were likely not enjoying themselves too much.

On the other hand, have you ever been part of a meeting where the energy was so powerful and in such abundance that you could feel it? Where you were more awake and participating in that meeting more than others? What did that feel like? What did people look like? What were people saying or doing? Likely, people in the meeting were engaged, focused and maybe even having a little fun while getting work done.

Oprah Winfrey had a quote from Jill Bolte Taylor, author of *My Stroke of Insight* framed on her office wall as a reminder to all who entered that stated, "You are responsible for the energy you bring into this space."

Imagine if we all took responsibility for the energy we brought into the meetings we attend. Imagine if, as meeting leaders, trainers or facilitators, we took responsibility for the energy we brought to those participating in our meetings, our trainings, and our work sessions. What a difference good energy can make!

So, then, why a little book about energizers? Well, we believe that no matter how interesting the subject, how skilled the facilitator, how long the duration, everyone needs an energy boost if they will be sitting longer than 10 minutes. Yes, ten minutes. Why ten? Because honestly, after about that time, we start to get antsy, start thinking about our to-do lists waiting for us back at our desks that we can't get to because, well, we're in a meeting! And research shows that we have hundreds of thoughts per minute and not always about the topic at hand! No one can argue with the current thinking in brain research that states that physical activity is not only important to our "physical" body but to our brain – our ability to think, solve problems, and grow and evolve as human beings is directly related to our physical activity (or lack thereof). The benefits of movement are endless – boosting the flow of oxygen to the brain, increasing our brain cells, regulating our breathing and heart rate, the list goes on and on. But, you get the point. Changing the "state" with physical or mental movement gets people's brains working more effectively and shifts them out of their preoccupations and, you guessed it, brings more energy to the space. And even if people are diligently focused on the topic at hand, it's still good to shake things up a bit, change the state to help our brains take a break and get more energy once we re-focus.

Simply put, the benefits of adding energizers to your meetings are endless – you can wake up drowsy meeting participants, shift the "energy level" to get better ideas flowing, have fun, help participants retain information better and have participants leaving fresher than when they walked in!

So, if you want to shake things up a bit and add a little fun and a lot more productivity to your meetings, not only will those who attend your meetings thank you for the energy and fun you brought to it, but they will thank you for helping their brains grow! And even if we can't guarantee brain growth, we bet they will be more engaged, more lively, they will come up with better ideas and you know what, they may even start to look forward to going to your meetings!

The energizers in this book vary in duration, complexity and purpose. Most of them are fairly quick to do and with a few variations in certain instances, ALL of them can be used for just about any group size. Some require a little advanced planning on your part, but not anything that will cause you too much extra work.

As a team, we like to look for inspiration wherever we go – whether we are traveling abroad, going out with friends, or working with our awesome clients. And the energizers in this book reflect that inspiration. We are always on the lookout for ways to make our own meetings more fun and for ways to engage those we teach and work with around the globe. We've curated these energizers from the inspiration we've gotten from others or found while exploring the world around us. So, to that end, these energizers come from multiple sources. Many we created ourselves, some we've modified after having participated in them at different events, meetings and training programs.

Our team has participated in and facilitated every energizer in here and this little book reflects what has worked best over the years after some trial and error and participant feedback. Don't worry, no one ever got hurt doing these energizers, although some ceiling tiles needed to be replaced a few times. (See if you can guess which energizer caused THAT problem!) Just remember to trust yourself, trust the group, and know your audience.

We'd love to hear from you about how these worked for you, what variations you may have used that worked well and of course, share any new energizers you have that we can share with our community! Check us out on www. dxdpartners.com or email us at info@dxdpartners.com to share.

That's it. That's all. Time to get stimulated! Time to get energized! Here's to meetings that are more fun, more focused and simply more fabulous!

Jeannine and Andrew

I-SCREAM

How To	Time Required	Tips
• Ask the group to form one large circle (if there are more than 20 participants, use two circles and modify accordingly). • Tell the group that the object of this energizer is to be the last one (or two) standing. • Tell the group that on the count of three, everyone must look at someone else in the circle. They must look at someone's eyes – not the floor or ground or the wall. • Tell the group that if that SAME person is looking back at you, you both scream and are out of the game. If the person you are looking at is not looking back at you, then you go on to the next round. • For the next and subsequent rounds each person must look at another person (they cannot generate a pattern where they continue to look at the same person each time who isn't looking back at them). • Continue until there are two people standing. Both are winners.	15 minutes	If you have more than 20 people, divide the large group into smaller groups and when the sizes are more manageable, merge the two groups into one to continue to play.

What Kind of Animal?

How To	Time Required	Tips
• Ask the group to stand up and think of their favorite animal. It can be a farm animal, wild animal or domesticated animal. Ask them not to tell anyone which animal they selected. • Without talking, the group's task is to arrange themselves from the smallest to the largest animal. They can use only non-verbal communication to help arrange themselves. • After the group has arranged themselves in what they feel is the correct size order, ask each person (starting from the small end of the line) to announce their animal. • Chances are the group will be 95% arranged correctly with some tweaking as people reveal their animals.	10 minutes	This is good for most sized groups; with groups larger than 40, you might want to make two groups.

Notes, Deep Thoughts, Scribbles, and Doodles

Wrap Dance

How To	Time Required	Tips
• Arrange long strips of bubble wrap on the floor. Each person should have one 18-inch (or so) strip in front of them. • Ask participants to NOT step on the bubbles until you give them the instruction to do so. • Find a funky, upbeat dance song on your playlist to get ready to play (we like "Everybody Dance Now" by CC Music Factory). • Tell the group that when you start the music, they can start "dancing" and pop the bubbles. • Start the music and watch people get really into popping all the bubbles and of course, the music!	5 minutes	This can be done with 5 to 500 people! We've done it! It's a very fun and always appropriate energizer in our experience. The large sized bubble wrap works the best for this energizer. Give participants a quick break before you do this so you can set up the room without them seeing what you are doing. This is a great energizer to save for the end of a meeting or event – people leave with smiles on their faces and lots of energy!

Name That Tune

How To	Time Required	Tips
<ul><li>Keep your play list out from the last energizer (Wrap Dance!) and test your group's music saavy!</li><li>Play 5 – 8 ish seconds of a song for participants to hear.</li><li>Whoever knows the tune calls out the name and the artist; if they got it right, move on to the next, if not, continue until someone gets it.</li><li>Chances are there will be multiple people calling out the correct name of the song – so this is less of a contest and more of a fun, quick burst of energy to turn up the vibe!</li></ul>	It varies – it can take less than 5 minutes or it can take longer. It ultimately depends on how many tunes you decide to play.	It's best to set this up in advance so you have a playlist ready to go and don't have to fumble with it while you are doing the energizer. Typically 5 – 8 songs are enough to give people the mental break they need to get back on task. Use a variety of tunes (genres, artists and decades!) so everyone has a chance to participate based on their musical tastes and history. Classical, rock, hip-hop, pop, music from the 50s, 60s, 70s, etc. You get the picture!

Notes, Deep Thoughts, Scribbles, and Doodles

Shoe Toss

How To	Time Required	Tips
• Ask participants to follow you to an open area in your building or hotel. Outside works great on a beautiful day! • Tell them that they will be playing a game called "shoe toss" and that the object of the game is to get their shoe as close to an object (or inside that object if it is a box or some type of container) as possible to be the winner. The object can be a basket, bucket, cone, chair, box, etc. – nearly anything can work so long as it's not breakable! • Each person lines up behind a specified marker (you set the spot where they will toss from and everyone tosses their shoe from that same spot). • Each person gets their shoe to the edge of their foot and without using their hands kicks the shoe in the direction of the target. • Everyone leaves their shoe where it lands until everyone has had a chance to shoe toss so you can clearly see who got it closest (or in!) the set target. • After everyone has tossed his/her shoe, see whose shoe is closest. • Award a fun prize for the winner!	15 – 25 minutes (depending on size)	Find a spot where you won't do too much damage to walls, ceiling tiles, etc. Outside is best, if possible, weather permitting but we've done this many times inside with relatively little damage!

Freeze-Frame

How To	Time Required	Tips
• Blast the music (seeing a theme here?) and get people up from their seats. • Tell the group they will have a chance to let off some steam and get some energy by dancing! But, the trick is, they can only dance when the music is playing. When the music stops, they must freeze in whatever position they find themselves and not move – or they are out of the game! • A variation of this is to play the childhood game that many are familiar with called musical chairs. You line up one less chair than there are people (so if there are 10 people, you line up 9 chairs) and when the music stops, everyone has to sit down in an empty chair. If there are no chairs left for a person, they are out of the game!	5 minutes	This is good for any sized group and really stirs up the energy. Be sure to vary the length of time you play the music so they don't anticipate the stop time.

Notes, Deep Thoughts, Scribbles, and Doodles

Mob

How To	Time Required	Tips
• Before engaging the group in this energizer, select one person to be "it." "It" does not reveal his/her identity to anyone else in the group. • When you and the group are ready, ask everyone to stand up (including "it" because he/she is not to be known to the group as different) and have everyone close their eyes. • Tell them that they are to go around the room and shake hands with everyone. But, there is one person in the room, who, if he or she shakes their hand, they will be eliminated. They will know they are eliminated because the person we are calling "it" will lightly scratch or tickle the hands of those whose hands they shake. • Tell the group if they get eliminated, they are not to identify who is "it" but to stop playing the game. As the group gets smaller, they may start to guess who "it" is (silently) and each person can try to avoid "it" by not shaking hands with him/her. • Ask the group to begin. • Once most or all but "it" have been eliminated the energizer ends.	20 minutes	This is best for smaller groups. With bigger groups it can go on forever!! You can modify and have two "its" to make things go more quickly. Make sure each "it" knows there is another "it" playing. You can either tell the "its" the identity of each other or you can have them find out as they are playing. You can make it so that the "its" can't eliminate each other (or that they can) that's up to you!

Stress Rub

How To	Time Required	Tips
• Everyone stands up and forms a circle. Ask everyone to face left and rub the shoulders of the person in front of them. • After 60 seconds or less they turn to the right and "return the favor" and rub the shoulders of the person who just rubbed their shoulders.	3 minutes	This is great for some relaxation after a long meeting or learning session when everyone's bodies and brains are fried! This is good for any sized group. Best for groups of people who are comfortable with one another or who are okay touching the shoulders of someone. You can always give people permission to not participate if they are uncomfortable.

Notes, Deep Thoughts, Scribbles, and Doodles

Sing a Song

How To	Time Required	Tips
• Prepare cards beforehand each with a popular song written on it (popular in that the majority of your audience would likely know the tune if they heard it – an example might be the tune "Take Me Out To The Ball Game"). • Break the group into smaller teams, if necessary, as this is best with smaller groups of about 8 – 10 people in each group). • Each person has a chance to pick a card with a song on it and that person has to HUM the tune of the song (no words) until her team members guess the correct tune. • Continue until all participants have had a chance to HUM their tune.	15 – 20 minutes	A slight variation is to have participants make up their own songs and not use prepared songs to play.

Stock Market

How To	Time Required	Tips
• The object of this fun, exciting, and for one author of this book, a little stressful but totally worth it energizer, is for participants to collect 8 of the same cards (not the same suit, but the same card number – 8 8's or 8 kings or 8 5's or 8 Aces, etc.) • Once you have sorted your cards and have several possible combinations of 8s (as described above) and the total number of cards you have available will give each person 8 cards to start the game with (these will be random cards and you need to shuffle the cards well) you can spread out the cards either on the floor in the back of the room or some empty space where people can select their cards. Put these cards face down so people cannot see what they've selected. • Ask everyone to select 8 cards. Remind them that they are looking to get 8 of the same card (8 4's, 8 Queens, etc.). How they play is to first organize the random cards they selected to see if they have a bit of a start (maybe they already randomly picked up 3 4's or 4 Queens). They need to trade with someone else the number of cards they NEED. So, if I have 4 Queens and decide I'm going to try to win with Queens, I'll shout out "I need four. I need four." In this example, I can only trade with someone if they, too, are looking to get rid of four cards. Once I've traded, I may only need 2 cards next so I'll say "I need 2" until I find someone also looking to trade two cards. The group continues trading in this fashion until someone gets the set of eight cards. That person wins the round!	25 minutes	You really need to be organized for this one! Make sure you prepare the cards in advance. You'll need 8 cards per person (but NOT 8 perfect sets per person because not everyone should be able to get a winning hand). Advanced math skills preferred. ☺ Check out a video of this energizer with a client from Paris, France on our website https://www.dxdpartners.com/contact

Notes, Deep Thoughts, Scribbles, and Doodles

Energy Tank

How To	Time Required	Tips
• Create an imaginary (or real!) line on the floor in your space. Tell the group that this is the "energy tank line." • The idea for this energizer is to gauge the group to see how "energized" everyone is at a given point in the time you are together. • Each person is to stand on the energy tank line at the place where they feel their energy is at that moment. Towards one side of this line (be sure to designate sides and communicate that to the group) participants who are full of energy go there. These are the ones who have a 100% full tank – they are ready to go and are the "feeling great" crowd. Towards the other side of the line, these are the people with not as much energy – an empty tank and the "ready to take a nap" crowd. And then there is the in between crowd. Not sleepy but not raring to go either! • Once participants have chosen a spot, take a mental note of how many people are feeling like they've got a full tank, medium tank and a low tank. Adjust how you proceed with your meeting accordingly. • Once everyone is at their spot, thank them and let them know you will check in with them again later in the day (if you say this, be sure to do it) and they can take their seats.	5 minutes or less	This is good for all sized groups and gives the facilitator a quick "pulse" of the energy in the room. This energizer can be done anytime during a meeting or event and even multiple times to keep a pulse of the energy in the room.

Story Telling

How To	Time Required	Tips
• Ask the group to get into pairs. Tell them to decide which person in the pair will be Person A and which will be Person B. Each person in the pair will have a turn to be Person A, the "random word thrower-outer" and Person B the "storyteller." • Person A (the random word thrower-outer) asks Person B to make up a story. The story can be about anything – food, travel, family, work, etc. • Person B starts to tell the story and after about 60 seconds, Person A inserts a random word and without skipping a beat, Person B needs to insert the random word into his/her story. This of course, will take the story on another trajectory, which is the point of this creative energizer! • Continue with a few random words (decide at the beginning how many random words should be interjected into the story at the beginning and communicate that to the group). Once the first person has finished the story, the pairs switch parts.	20 minutes	Put random words on index cards (one per card) to be able to hand out random words (or to make it easy, you can also purchase a deck of random words from us – contact us at info@ dxdpartners.com. You can also ask Person A to take 30 seconds to jot down a list of random words at the start of the energizer. You can do this with groups of 3 people as well as pairs. In this scenario, you can have two people throwing out random words to the storyteller and s/he has to incorporate both. Added fun! You can also use random props instead of words.

Notes, Deep Thoughts, Scribbles, and Doodles

Picture Perfect

How To	Time Required	Tips
• Hand out pre-printed copies of half-drawn pictures to everyone in the group. You can use things like a half drawing of an animal or half drawing of a nature scene, or half drawing of a famous building – you get the picture! • Ask each participant to complete the second part of the picture with all the creative energy they can muster. • Tell them to have fun with this and there are no right and no wrong answers. For example, if there is a half picture of a black and white cow, they can always complete the cow but it's colored purple or has polka dots, etc. or it can just be drawn the same as the other half. • Allow the majority of the time for the drawing, but allow a few minutes for some volunteers to share their artwork. You can also have them post their completed drawings around the room to remind them of their creativity.	10 – 15 minutes	A variation of this energizer is to get the group into pairs and one person starts the half picture and the other person completes the rest of the picture.

Pass the Ball

How To	Time Required	Tips
• Make sure you have a ball to throw (koosh, tennis, foam). Then, determine the goal for this energizer. Do you want participants to get to know one another better or review a key learning or make a commitment based on the meeting agenda or state their deliverable at the end of the meeting? Once you determine this, tell the group what the goal is and that is the object of this energizer. • Ask the group to stand in a circle and face one another. • Tell them that you will throw the ball to someone and they will start. Once they've stated the goal of the energizer, they will pass the ball to someone else in the circle. • A small "twist" to this energizer is that, as a group, they need to remember the pattern of how the ball gets thrown. Tell them that after they do this they will have to throw the ball back around in the order that was started at the beginning. • Begin by throwing the ball to someone in the group. That person starts the energizer. They state their name and then the goal (review learning, deliverable, something about themselves, etc.). Then they throw the ball to the next person (whoever they would like to throw it to). • The next person states their goal and throws it to the next person, and so on. • This continues in this way until everyone has had the chance to participate and with the last person, he or she throws it back to the first. • Now, the group just throws the ball around in the same pattern as before – no need to state anything this time around. See if the group can get the pattern correct!	10 minutes	This is good for large and small groups. To make this more difficult (read – more brain power!) you can have each person repeat what was said before. This works well with smaller groups and in situations where you want them to get to know one another better. So, if that is your goal, the energizer might start off something like this after throwing the ball to the first person: "I'm Sally and I'm originally from New York." Now Sally throws to the next person who says, "I'm James and I come from a family of 8 and that's Sally from New York." Now James throws to someone who says, "I'm Larry and I play guitar. That was James from a family of 8 and that's Sally from New York." And the process repeats from there.

Notes, Deep Thoughts, Scribbles, and Doodles

Tangled

How To	Time Required	Tips
• Ask the group to stand up in a circle facing each other. • Tell them that they are to take one of their hands and grab another person's hand and take their second hand and grab a different person's hand. • What will be created is a tangled web of people and hands. • Once everyone is holding the hands of two different people in the circle, tell them that the object of this energizer is to "untangle" themselves without detaching from those they are tangled with. They cannot break the tangle by letting go of the hands they are holding. • Allow time for the group to manage untangling. Most groups can do this after awhile. But once in awhile a team will really struggle. As the facilitator, you can allow them to decide as a group, which hands they should free to allow them to succeed. Either way it's fun and they have pumped up the energy level!	20 minutes	Best with groups no larger than 10 – 15 people. You can always break larger groups into smaller groups of this size.

Forbidden Words

How To	Time Required	Tips
• Break the group into pairs. • One person in the pair will have the "forbidden" words cards (Person A) and the other person will be the guesser (Person B). • Person A (with the forbidden words) tries to describe the word without saying the word or any of the related words on the list (that the facilitator buys or assembles before hand). • For example, let's say the word you are trying to get your partner to say is SNOW. The forbidden words (in addition of course to the word snow) could be words like frosty, winter, white, skiing, cold, ball, etc. You need about 6 "forbidden" words for each word you want to have pairs guess. • After a few rounds, have the pairs switch roles and be ready for a lot of laughs!	15 – 20 minutes	A variation is to use props. Just make sure that the "guessing" partner doesn't see the prop. Forbidden Word cards can be purchased by contacting us at info@dxdpartners.com or the facilitator can make them up him or herself before the meeting.

Notes, Deep Thoughts, Scribbles, and Doodles

Say, What?

How To	Time Required	Tips
• Break the group into smaller teams of 3 – 5 people in each (depending on your total number in the group). • Hand each team a list of foreign words (you can look up some words right from the internet). The trick is to have words from many different languages (or at least a few) and maybe even some uncommon languages (Hungarian, anyone?). You might give a few "easy" ones that many people might know. In the NY area, using "Gracias" or "Hola" as a word to translate is one that even if no one in the group speaks Spanish, out of a group of 3 – 5 people, someone would likely know. • The teams' challenge is to translate as many of the words as possible. The team that translates the most words wins. Something. Anything. Maybe a trip abroad?	10 minutes	Search for everyday words in the language (or languages) of your choice. You can easily find many. Or dust off your old foreign language dictionary from college and search the old fashioned way! You can also purchase a list of foreign words (in several different languages) from us. Contact us at info@dxdpartners.com.

In the Bag

How To	Time Required	Tips
• This energizer can be done in large or small groups. Make sure you have enough props for the number of groups/people you have. • With eyes closed, each person selects something out of the bag and the object is for that person to figure out what it is by "feeling" it. • When they guess, they can look to see if they are right. • Of course, you can use the traditional stuff like coins, pens, cups. But to make it a little more interesting, you can use paper clips that have been stretched out of their original shape, or silly putty or something fun like that! • Blindfolds work well with this – adds a little drama!	10 minutes (depends on your group size)	Use your imagination to come up with some different stuff – but remember, know your audience. You wouldn't want to offend anyone!

Stretch it Out

How To	Time Required	Tips
<ul><li>Ask the group to stand up.</li><li>Once they stand, ask them to follow along with what you do.</li><li>Give them the following instruction: First, stretch your arms over your head and hold for 10 seconds. Then, take your arms and stretch to the right side of the room and hold. Then take your arms back up to the center. Then slowly drop both your hands down to the sides of your body. Take a deep breath and then another. Now, take your arms up to the center again, hold and then stretch to the left side. Hold each of these stretches for about 30 – 60 seconds.</li><li>You can add other stretches that you might do from your yoga classes or before you run or workout.</li><li>A variation is to have someone in the group lead the rest of you through some stretch routine (maybe there's a fitness instructor in your group?)</li><li>Do this for a few rounds until everyone seems to have gained a bit of energy!</li></ul>	5 minutes	Remind your group to breathe while they are doing the stretches. Any good yoga teacher will tell you that it brings you a better stretch and oxygen to your cells – and therefore giving you more energy! Be sure to tell the group to do ONLY what they are comfortable with and not to push. If anyone has an injury or recent surgery, they may want to opt out of this one this time around. The idea is to increase energy flow and wake up a bit – not to pull a muscle!

Mantra Madness

How To	Time Required	Tips
• Have the group get into smaller teams of 4 – 5 people each (if you only have 4 – 5 people in the group to start off, then one team is fine). A way to break the large group down can be either random or by a particular job type or project team or specific tasks that people are assigned to. • Each team is to create a mantra – simply put a mantra is a verbal or visual formula to remind a team of its goals and purpose. It becomes part of the team's psychic energy and should resonate with everyone. • If there's time, you can take this a step further and ask them to design a visual representation of the mantra or a symbol that quickly communicates the mantra. • Have the teams post their written/visual mantras and go around the room to have each team present their mantra and why/how they came up with the mantra they did.	25 – 30 minutes	Teams can "act out" their mantras for added fun and a lot of laughs. This is great for team alignment sessions or goal setting with intact teams. If the large group wants to come up with just one mantra, you can make it competitive by having small teams work, then present to one another in the most creative way possible to "sell" their mantra. Then the whole group votes on the one mantra that they all want for their overall mantra. Some mantra examples: Let's get to next; Foresight, Focus and Fortune; Grow to Go, Be Like Water

Notes, Deep Thoughts, Scribbles, and Doodles

20 Questions

How To	Time Required	Tips
• When you were a kid you probably played this game on a long car ride to visit your Aunt Marge! Well, this is even more fun now that you are a grown up! • Pair people up in twos. One person (the thinker) in the pair thinks of a person, place or thing. The other person (the questioner) can ask 20 questions to find out what the thinker is thinking! • The thinker can only answer yes or no. That's it. No lengthy conversations here! • Have the pairs switch roles and do another round!	10 minutes	Although it is unlikely you will need it, be prepared with some ideas for people, places and things in case someone gets stuck. A variation on this that works especially well with in-tact teams is for the people, places, or things to be related to their work. A colleague, a building location around the world, specific work processes or tasks.

Many Uses

How To	Time Required	Tips
• This energizer asks participants to use their creativity to think of as many uses as possible for a given object. You can think of the objects yourself (and bring them with you) or have the individuals come up with the objects themselves. • You can have people work individually, in small groups or in pairs. • Instruct the group: In the next 2 minutes, come up with as many alternate uses for this object (paper clip, football, earplugs, etc.) as you can. Or you can ask them to come up with a certain number (come up with 99 alternate uses for this object). • You can also use this energizer and apply this to something related to their work. If they are in the retail or consumer products business, perhaps they can come up with 99 different uses for their XYZ brand of pantyhose or sippy cups or chocolate. • The ideas may amaze the group, and who knows, may be their next innovation!	5 – 10 minutes	Make it a competition – the person, pair or team who comes up with the most ideas wins a small prize (maybe a box of paperclips!). Or the person, pair, or team who comes up with the craziest, most creative ideas wins. Of course you will have to plan your give-aways ahead of time and have enough for all who win!

Notes, Deep Thoughts, Scribbles, and Doodles

Songwriting

How To	Time Required	Tips
• Break participants into small teams. • Each group writes a song to the beat of a familiar tune (e.g., *Margaritaville* by Jimmy Buffet or another song that most in the group will be familiar with). • Tell each team what the theme or the content of the song should be focused on. For example, the focus could be on key learnings from a workshop, introductions of the members of the group and one interesting fact about them, or something specifically related to the meeting content. • Each team performs the song they wrote. • And prizes for everyone! Each team worked hard and probably had a lot of laughs!	30 – 40 minutes	Each team can do a different tune, or different content to mix it up. Bring in some instruments so people can also play along to the beat! A variation on this energizer is for the teams to write poems instead of a song.

Choosing Sides

How To	Time Required	Tips
• Ask the group to stand up and designate two sides of the room you are in. • Tell the group that you will be asking them to make a choice based on their preferences and to walk to the side of the room that you indicate for that particular preference. • For example, you might ask: Beach or Mountains? For those who choose the beach, go to the back of the room. For those who choose mountains, go to the front. • Other possible preference choices are: moon or sun; siblings or only child; sweet or salty; half full or half empty; tea or coffee; romance or thriller; snow or rain; white wine or red wine, etc. Add your own! • Add some that have to do with the content of the meeting to have participants "vote" with their feet!	10 minutes	This is a great way to get to know people in a group better. So, it's ideal for introductions with new team members or even team building so that teams who have worked together for a long time can get to know one another more in depth.

Notes, Deep Thoughts, Scribbles, and Doodles

Unexpected Guests

How To	Time Required	Tips
• Tell the group that they will have the opportunity to cultivate their creativity by brainstorming many possibilities given a specific scenario. • Give the group the scenario: You come home from work and pull into your driveway and sitting on your driveway is (insert whatever you want them to brainstorm – a circus clown, your mother in law, a rock star, a zoo animal, 100 rats, etc.) • Tell the group that they have 2 minutes to brainstorm what you would do. • After time, have everyone share what they would do and have a lot of laughs!	10 minutes	You can give different sides of the room different scenarios to mix it up a bit. You can also break the groups into teams for a team challenge.

Imagine

How To	Time Required	Tips
• Break the group into small groups of 4 – 5 people each. • Give each small group a stack of "imagine" cards* and some paper and pens. • Ask each small group to choose one person to be "it" and another person to select a card from the stack. This person (who selects the card) will read the card aloud to everyone. • For example, if Max, on our team is "it" and I pick the card for the team, here's how it might play out. I read the card and the card might say, "Imagine _____ (I would insert Max's name) were a movie. What movie would she/he be? Then list the five possibilities under the Imagine statement. So, in this case the five possibilities are: a drama, a comedy, a horror show, a love story, an action adventure. • Each team member writes down what they think "it" (in this case, MAX) would chose for himself. "It" (Max in our example) writes down his selection and each other team member does the same. • You can assign points – if someone choses the same as "it," they get one point. If a person choses something other than what "it" chose for him or herself, "it" (in this case, Max) gets the point. • Do this for several rounds so that everyone has at least one time to be "it."	15 – 25 minutes (depends on the size of the small groups)	*You guessed it, Imagine cards are available by contacting us at info@ dxdpartners.com. If you prefer to make your own cards, you can easily put some together! This is a great "getting to know" you type energizer. It's fun, fast- moving and brings lots of laughs!

Notes, Deep Thoughts, Scribbles, and Doodles

Trivia

How To	Time Required	Tips
• This energizer can be used with the large group or you can break the group into small teams for some added competition. • If you use with the large group, select a card and ask the question on the card. You can either make up your own trivia cards or you can purchase by contacting us at info@dxdpartners.com. • Once someone gets the answer correct, move on to the next card. • Continue until you run out of time or cards or both!	5 minutes	Trivia questions can be about random topics or you can construct specific "trivia" questions related to the company or the team project. For new employees, this can be a fun way to get to know the company history!

Charades

How To	Time Required	Tips
• Just like the game you played at your family reunion! Here is a version you can use with groups of any size. • Pre-make charades papers (or visit us at www.dxdpartners.com for FREE charades papers that you can cut out to use) and cut and fold to put into a box or hat for people to pick without seeing what they are picking. • Split the large group into two teams. Each team member gets a turn to "act out" the charades slip of paper they select from the box or the hat. They cannot use any words – only gestures, movement, non-verbal communication. • Consider prizes for best acting!	25 minutes	Use this energizer when you have a good amount of time to devote to it. It works particularly well before lunch (when energy is typically low) or before the end of the day.

Notes, Deep Thoughts, Scribbles, and Doodles

Picture This

How To	Time Required	Tips
• Give everyone in your group a marker (we like black Sharpie markers) and some colored 8 ½ x 11-inch paper. • Ask each person to sketch a word that is related to the work you are doing or a concept you are trying to teach or discuss. • For example, if you are trying to get a sense of how each person defines (or visualizes) the concept of "teambuilding" or "innovation" or "passion," state the word and have each person draw that on their paper. • This should be done quickly. The idea is to get a sketch, quick rendition, not a Picasso masterpiece. • Have everyone post their sketches and have a conversation about the differences and similarities across all of the drawings.	10 – 15 minutes	For repeat meetings (with the same meeting participants), it can be helpful to keep these sketches for the next meeting to remind everyone of the work that was done previously. You can even build on the sketches to see how people's definitions or perceptions may have changed.

Symbols

How To	Time Required	Tips
• Tell the group that their task is to go about the space (the meeting room, the hotel, the building, maybe even outside) to find an object that "symbolizes" who they are or what is important to them. • For example, one meeting participant found a penny while walking around outside at an offsite location. For her, this represented the fact that she was always able to see two sides of any issue, which helped her understand another person's perspective. • Allow enough time for people to explore a bit to find the "right" object. • Once participants have found their object, ask each person to share with the large group what the object is and how it symbolizes who they are or what is important to them.	15 – 20 minutes	This is a great "getting to know you" type activity as it creates conversation. It's best for groups up to 20 people.

Notes, Deep Thoughts, Scribbles, and Doodles

Four Corners

How To	Time Required	Tips
• Take four pieces of flip chart paper and put a quote on each. Quotes can be related to the meeting content or can be random. Quotes can be from all the same people or several different people. Post the flip chart with quote in each corner of the room so people need to walk around gallery style to read them all. • Ask the group to go around the room and read each quote. After they've read each quote, ask them to stand next to the quote that resonates most for them. Depending on the size of the group, likely others will gather around the same quote. • As people gather around the quotes, have them discuss with one another why that quote resonates with them – why they chose that quote. If only one person is left by a quote, a good role for the meeting leader or facilitator is to go over to them and discuss with them so they are not alone. • Once the groups who are gathered around each quote have had time to discuss the quotes, ask them to pick a spokesperson to give a summary as to what the common reasons for picking that quote were, or themes that emerged in conversation or what resonated for them as a whole group.	15 minutes	You can use your own quotes or check out some of our favorites to borrow at www.dxdpartners.com. You can have people guess who said each quote for some added fun and competition!

Owner of the Keys

How To	Time Required	Tips
• Ask participants to take out their keys (to their car, their home, or something that they carry keys for) and place them in either a bucket (that gets passed around) or a designated spot in the room. • Once everyone has given over their keys, ask each participant to select a different set of keys. • Now that they have someone else's keys, ask them to jot down on a piece of paper what they can tell about the owner of those keys based on the keys and/or the key chain. • Suggest things such as gender, personality, hobbies, the purpose of the key(s), if they are car keys what type of make, model and year of the car (if applicable), if they are house keys, can you guess the style of the house the person lives in – does this person live alone, with others, etc. You get the point! • Tell the group to have some fun with this and see how creative they can get about the personalities of the owner of the keys. • Once they've had about 3 – 5 minutes to make the list, have each person read their list out loud and chose who they think the owner of the keys is. Others in the group can also guess if the person making the list didn't guess correctly. • The real owner of the keys identifies him or herself after the guessing is complete.	10 – 20 minutes	To enhance this energizer, you can have the key owners discuss whether or not some of the items on the list were true. This can be used as a good introduction energizer for people who may not know one another.

Notes, Deep Thoughts, Scribbles, and Doodles